What Are the Parts of Government?

By William David Thomas

D0912041

 **Gareth Stevens**
Publishing

Please visit our web site at www.garethstevens.com. For a free catalog describing Gareth Stevens Publishing's list of high-quality books, call 1-800-542-2595 (USA) or 1-800-387-3178 (Canada). Gareth Stevens Publishing's fax: 1-877-542-2596

Library of Congress Cataloging-in-Publication Data

Thomas, William, 1947-
    What are the parts of government? / William David Thomas.
        p. cm.—(My American government)
    Includes bibliographical references and index.
    ISBN-10: 0-8368-8862-6   ISBN-13: 978-0-8368-8862-1 (lib. bdg.)
    ISBN-10: 0-8368-8867-7   ISBN-13: 978-0-8368-8867-6 (softcover)
    1. United States—Politics and government—Juvenile literature.   I. Title.
    JK40.T56   2008
    320.473—dc22   2007026511

This edition first published in 2008 by
Gareth Stevens Publishing
A Weekly Reader® Company
1 Reader's Digest Road
Pleasantville, NY 10570-7000 USA

Copyright © 2008 by Gareth Stevens, Inc.

Senior Managing Editor: Lisa M. Guidone
Creative Director: Lisa Donovan
Cover Designer: Jeannie Friedman
Interior Designer: Yin Ling Wong
Photo Researchers: Kimberly Babbitt and Charlene Pinckney

Picture Credits: Cover, title page: AP Photo/Ron Edmonds; p. 5 Shutterstock (3); p. 7 © Martin H. Simon/Corbis; p. 8 Pablo Martinez Monsivais/AP; p. 11 John Raoux/AP; pp. 12-13 Shutterstock; p. 15 Yuri Gripas/AFP/Getty Images; p. 18 © Ron Sachs/Corbis; p. 20 Photograph by Steve Petteway, Collection of the Supreme Court of the U.S.; p. 21 Charles Ommanney/ Getty Images; p. 23 Carl Iwasaki/Time & Life Pictures/Getty Images; p. 25 Spc. Wes Landrum, 50th Public Affairs Detachment; p. 27 © MedioImages/Corbis; p. 29 Shutterstock

Printed in the United States of America

2 3 4 5 6 7 8 9 10 09 08

Contents

Words in the glossary appear in **bold** type
the first time they are used in the text.

CHAPTER 1

★

Government Basketball

Kylie really liked basketball. Her older sister, Kelcey, was a star on the high school team. Kelcey was also a star in the classroom, and she was helping Kylie get ready for a social studies test.

"I just don't get it!" said Kylie.

"Well look," said Kelcey, "the government is a lot like basketball."

"You have got to be kidding!"

"I'm serious," said Kelcey. "The **U.S. Constitution** is the highest law in the land. It sets up three parts, or branches, of government. They're the **executive branch**, the **legislative branch**, and the **judicial branch**. Each one has a different job to do."

"Which one is the point guard?" joked Kylie.

Kelcey smiled but kept talking.

"The executive branch is like the coach. The coach is the chief executive."

"You mean the coach is like the president?" Kylie asked.

"In some ways," replied Kelcey. "But there is more to the executive branch than just the president. Then there is the legislative branch."

"What's that?"

"That's Congress," said Kelcey. "They're sort of like the team. The players are picked from all the kids in the high school. The coach is important, but the players are the ones who have to take action. Without them, there is no game."

"Well, what about that other branch?" Kylie wondered.

LEGISLATIVE BRANCH
*Congress (Senate and
House of Representatives)*
Makes the Laws

EXECUTIVE BRANCH
*President, Vice President,
and other officials*
Enforces the Laws

JUDICIAL BRANCH
*Supreme Court
and lower courts*
Interprets the Laws

"The judicial branch. They're like the referees," Kelcey explained. "They make sure that both the coach and the players follow the rules."

"Okay, okay," said Kylie. "The executive branch is the president and some others. They're the coaches. The legislative branch is Congress. They're the team. And the referees are the judicial branch."

"Good shot," said Kelcey. "Of course, all three branches have to work together."

"How?" Kylie asked.

"Just like in basketball," said Kelcey. "At practice Megan and Chantelle came up with a new play, but Coach Sharpe said…"

"Hey!" Their father interrupted. "What's all this basketball talk? You're supposed to be working on social studies."

"But Dad," said Kylie, "we are!"

"Yeah, right. Next you'll tell me the dog ate your homework."

★

CHAPTER 2

The Executive Branch

"So the coach is like the president," said Kylie.

"Yes," said Kelcey. "But a team needs more than a coach. It also needs bus drivers, score keepers, people to schedule the games, and lots more. In the same way, the president needs the executive branch."

The President

The president heads up the executive branch of government. The U.S. Constitution says the president must "take care that the laws be faithfully executed." To enforce the laws, the president has certain powers.

- As chief executive, the president oversees the major offices of the U.S. government. The president chooses the people who lead those offices.

- The president is commander-in-chief of the armed forces, which includes the Army, Navy, Air Force, and Marines.

THE STATE OF THE UNION

The president must "from time to time give to Congress information of the State of the Union." That rule is in the Constitution. Today, the president's "state of the union" address, or speech, is a big event. Each year, the president outlines the plans for the country in a televised speech. Many years ago, presidents just wrote a letter to Congress.

President George W. Bush welcomes Queen Elizabeth II of England to America in May 2007. Meeting leaders of other countries is one of the president's duties.

- The president can make **treaties** with foreign countries.
- The president may **veto**, or reject, a **bill** passed by Congress.
- As head of state, the president is a symbol of the nation. The president represents the country at home and abroad.

The president has great powers. But those powers are controlled by the Constitution. This system is called "checks and balances." It keeps any part of the government from becoming too powerful. For example, the president commands the armed forces. However, only Congress can declare war. The president can make treaties with foreign countries. But the treaties must be approved by Congress before they can go into effect.

The president meets with his top advisers. From left to right: President George W. Bush talks with Vice President Dick Cheney, Secretary of State Condoleezza Rice, and Secretary of Defense Robert Gates.

The Vice President

The vice president is the second highest-ranking person in the government. The vice president becomes president if:

- the president dies in office (this has happened eight times)
- the president resigns (this has only happened once)
- the president is removed from office by Congress (this has never happened)

The Constitution gives the vice president one responsibility—president of the Senate. If a vote in the Senate ends in a tie, the vice president votes to break the tie. The vice president also works with leaders in Congress and helps the president make decisions.

Long ago, there was no vice presidential candidate on the ballot. People only voted for the president. The person with the most votes became president. The person in second place became the vice president. This was changed by the Twelfth Amendment to the Constitution. Since 1804, people have voted for the president and vice president as a team.

The Cabinet

The leaders of the largest government departments make up the president's **cabinet**. Cabinet members are chosen by the president and approved by the Senate. These leaders are called secretaries. Each secretary manages his or her department and advises the president. The Secretary of State deals with foreign countries. The Secretary of Defense works with the military. The Secretary of Transportation looks after roads, airports, and railroads.

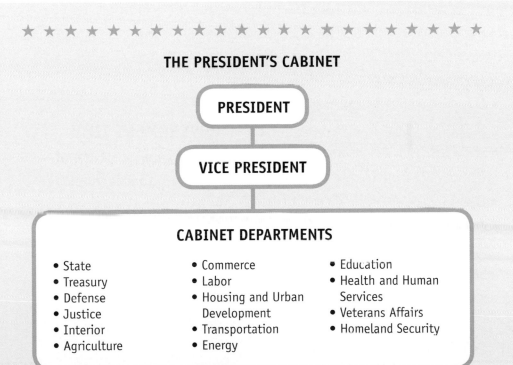

★ ★

THE PRESIDENT'S CABINET

PRESIDENT

VICE PRESIDENT

CABINET DEPARTMENTS

- State
- Treasury
- Defense
- Justice
- Interior
- Agriculture
- Commerce
- Labor
- Housing and Urban Development
- Transportation
- Energy
- Education
- Health and Human Services
- Veterans Affairs
- Homeland Security

★ ★

Next in Line

Who replaces the president if he or she dies or cannot work? First, of course, is the vice president. But if the vice president cannot, then next in line is the Speaker of House. This is the leader of the **House of Representatives**. Fourth in line is the *President Pro Tempore* of the **Senate**. This is usually a senator from the party with the most seats in the Senate who has been in office for many years. Next is the Secretary of State, then the Secretary of the Treasury, the Secretary of Defense, and the Attorney General. He or she is followed by other cabinet members.

Federal Agencies

Many **federal** agencies are part of the executive branch, too. These agencies advise the president on such things as national security, illegal drugs, trade, the **budget**, and science. Some of these agencies are:

- the Central Intelligence Agency (CIA)
- the National Aeronautics and Space Administration (NASA)
- the Environmental Protection Agency (EPA)

Altogether, nearly three million people work in the executive branch. With the president, they "take care that the laws be faithfully executed."

GOVERNMENT TIME

The National Institute of Standards and Technology is part of the executive branch. One of its duties is to keep track of the official time in the United States. You can check the time at **www.nist.time.gov**.

THE SECRET SERVICE

You may know about the Secret Service from movies. Its agents protect the president. But when the Secret Service began, in 1865, its job was to protect money! At that time, nearly one-third of all money in use in America was **counterfeit**. President McKinley was shot and killed in 1901. After that, the Secret Service began to protect the president. Today the Secret Service does that and more. It investigates many kinds of crimes dealing with electronics and money.

The space shuttle *Endeavor* is ready to launch from Cape Canaveral, Florida. NASA runs the U.S. space program and is one of the federal agencies that are part of the executive branch.

★

CHAPTER 3

The Legislative Branch

"So what's the big deal about Congress?" asked Kylie. "I mean, the president runs the government, right?"

"It's the president's job to enforce the laws," reminded Kelcey, "but Congress creates the laws."

The Powers of Congress

Congress is the legislative branch of the government. That means it is the law-making branch. Congress meets in the U.S. Capitol in Washington, D.C.

Congress does much more than make laws. The Constitution gives this branch of government many powers. These include the following powers:

- collect taxes and pay debts
- borrow money
- control trade between the United States and other nations and between the states
- print money
- make post offices and roads
- approve people that the president wants to hire
- declare war

Senate

One Congress, Two Houses

Congress has two parts, or houses. The House of Representatives has 435 members. Each state has a different number of representatives. The number depends on the state's population. California has fifty-three representatives. Vermont has only one. Members of the House serve a term that lasts two years. They can be re-elected many times.

The other house of Congress is the Senate. There are one hundred senators. Each state has two senators, no matter what

Notice the flagpoles on each wing of the Capitol. When the Senate is in session, a flag flies over north wing (on the left). When the House meets, a flag flies over the south wing (on the right). When either house meets at night, a light shines in the dome.

House

IMPEACHMENT

Congress has the power to remove the president from office. First, the House must vote to accuse the president of an action that could justify removal from office. This is called **impeachment**. If this happens, a trial is held in the Senate. At the end of the trial, the senators vote. Two-thirds of them must vote yes to remove the president. Two presidents, Andrew Johnson and Bill Clinton, have been impeached. Neither was removed from office.

the population. Each senator serves a term of six years. They too may be re-elected.

There are checks and balances in Congress, too. Each house has different powers. For example, only the House can suggest laws to raise money. The Senate can't do that. For any law to pass, however, both houses must agree to it.

SENATOR ASTRONAUT

John Glenn served four terms as U.S. senator from Ohio. Before that, he was an astronaut. Glenn was the third American ever to fly in space. In 1962, he became the first American to orbit Earth. He went back into space on the shuttle *Discovery* in 1998. Glenn was then 77 years old. He was the oldest person—and the only senator—to have flown in space. He retired from the Senate the next year.

Nancy Pelosi, a representative from California, greets visitors to Washington, D.C. In 2007, Pelosi became the first woman Speaker of the House. The Speaker is next in line for the presidency, after the vice president.

Three Jobs

Members of Congress have three main jobs. They help make or change laws. They oversee the executive branch. And finally, they speak for the people of their state.

Making a law is complicated. When people in Congress go about proposing laws, they look at older laws. They talk to people who want the law. They also talk to people who may oppose it. Sometimes they talk to the president, who can also suggest laws. Both parts of Congress must agree to a new law, so members of both houses also talk to each other.

The second job of Congress is **oversight**. This is part of the checks and balances system. Oversight means that Congress watches over the other parts of the government. One way Congress does this is through the Government Accountability Office (GAO). Workers in this large office watch all of the agencies in the executive branch. Congress also has special oversight committees. One of them makes sure that medicines are safe to use. Other committees watch over the military, the banking industry, airlines, and trade with foreign countries.

The third job of each person in Congress is to help meet the needs of his or her state. States don't all want the same things, of course. For example, products made from corn are now being added to gasoline. This helps Americans use less gas. In Iowa and Nebraska, where large amounts of corn are grown, this is very important. The senators and representatives from those states want laws saying these corn products must be used in cars. Other states have different needs. Arizona needs more water. Florida wants its citrus business to grow. Their senators and representatives try to pass laws that will help those states.

How a Bill Becomes a Law

Each year, Congress considers thousands of bills. A bill is like a first draft of a law. When a bill starts in the Senate, one or two senators write it. Then the bill goes to a committee of senators. The committee studies the bill. Then it may:

1. Send the bill back with no changes.
2. Make changes and send it back.
3. Table the bill. That means the committee just keeps the bill but doesn't do anything with it.

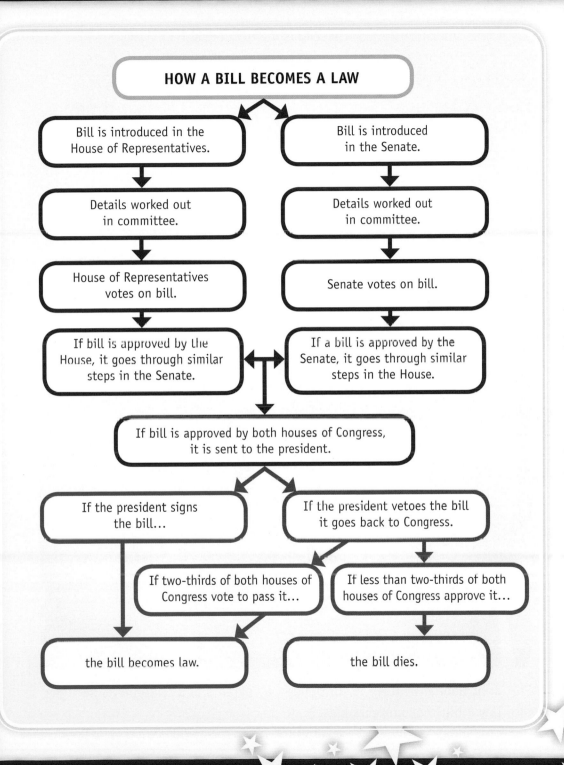

HOW A BILL BECOMES A LAW

Bill is introduced in the House of Representatives.

Bill is introduced in the Senate.

Details worked out in committee.

Details worked out in committee.

House of Representatives votes on bill.

Senate votes on bill.

If bill is approved by the House, it goes through similar steps in the Senate.

If a bill is approved by the Senate, it goes through similar steps in the House.

If bill is approved by both houses of Congress, it is sent to the president.

If the president signs the bill...

If the president vetoes the bill it goes back to Congress.

If two-thirds of both houses of Congress vote to pass it...

If less than two-thirds of both houses of Congress approve it...

the bill becomes law.

the bill dies.

If the bill isn't tabled, the bill is voted on by the whole Senate. If more than half of the Senators voting vote yes, the bill goes to the House of Representatives. There the bill goes to a House committee. They study it. If they make changes, the bill goes back to the Senate for approval. Then it comes back to the House again.

The House votes on the bill. If more than half of the members voting vote yes, the bill goes to the president. If the president signs the bill, it becomes a law. If the president vetoes (rejects) the bill, it goes back to Congress. This time, two-thirds of the House and the Senate must vote in favor of it. If they do, the bill becomes a law. If they don't, the bill dies.

President George W. Bush is surrounded by parents and children as he signs into law a bill that protects kids.

CHAPTER 4

★

The Judicial Branch

"Tell me again about the judicial branch," said Kylie.

"The judicial branch is like the referees," said Kelcey. "This branch makes sure that both the president and Congress follow the rules."

"What rules? Where are they?"

"The rules," said Kelcey, "are in the U.S. Constitution."

The Judicial Branch

The judicial branch of the government is all about laws. But it does not make laws. The judicial branch decides if laws have been broken. The judicial branch also makes sure that state and federal laws agree with the Constitution.

The judicial branch includes the federal court system. The court system has three levels. At the lowest level are the district courts. They hold trials for crimes against federal laws or property or for actions that may violate the Constitution. Above them are thirteen courts of **appeal**. These courts hear a case when lawyers disagree with the ruling in a district court. Finally there is the Supreme Court, in Washington, D.C.

The Supreme Court

The Supreme Court is the highest court in the United States. Its most important job is to interpret the U.S. Constitution. The

These are the nine justices of the Supreme Court in 2007. Back row (left to right) are Stephen Breyer, Clarence Thomas, Ruth Bader Ginsburg, and Samuel Alito. In the front row are (left to right) Anthony Kennedy, John Paul Stevens, Chief Justice John Roberts, Antonin Scalia, and David Souter.

Constitution was written more than two hundred years ago. The Court must decide how the rules in the Constitution apply to what happens today.

The Court can decide that a law is unconstitutional. If that happens, the law is nullified. That means it is no longer a law. The Court can also decide that actions taken by Congress or the president are unconstitutional. If so, those actions must stop.

There are no juries in the Supreme Court. There are nine judges, called **justices**. One of them is the chief justice. When the Court hears a case, all nine justices listen. They discuss the case. Then they vote. A simple majority—just five votes—is all that is needed to decide a case.

Supreme Court justices are chosen by the president. However, the Senate must approve the president's choices. It doesn't always do so. In 1987, President Ronald Reagan chose Robert Bork to serve as a justice. The Senate would not approve him. Once they are approved, justices serve until they die or retire. Most of them serve for many years.

The Supreme Court has made decisions about slavery, religion, and even presidential elections. The Court's rulings are often

SOME FAMOUS SUPREME COURT JUSTICES

These are some of the notable people who have served in the highest part of the judicial branch of government.

- **William Douglas** served for thirty-six years (1939–1975). That is the longest term in Supreme Court history.

- **Thurgood Marshall** served from 1967 to 1991. He was the first African American Supreme Court justice.

- **Sandra Day O'Connor** (right) was the first woman Supreme Court Justice. She served from 1981 until she retired in 2006.

controversial. The justices have to stay calm and think clearly. Oliver Wendell Holmes was a famous justice. He once said, "We are very quiet here, but it is the quiet of a storm center."

Famous Supreme Court Decisions

Marbury v. Madison (1803): The Court and the Constitution

President John Adams' term in office was nearly over. Before it ended, Adams named many people to government jobs. One of them was William Marbury. But when the new president, Thomas Jefferson, took office, he would not let Marbury serve. Marbury sued James Madison, who was Jefferson's Secretary of State. He claimed that, according to a law passed by Congress in 1789, he should have the job. The case reached the Supreme Court. The justices ruled that the 1789 law was unconstitutional. This was the first time that the Supreme Court reversed a law passed by Congress. This case made the judicial branch an equal partner in government, along with the executive and legislative branches.

Brown v. Board of Education (1954): Separate Schools

Oliver Brown was an African American. In the 1950s, he lived in Topeka, Kansas. The schools were **segregated**. Black children and white children could not attend the same schools. Brown wanted his daughter Linda to go to the white children's school. He took the school board to court. Brown's case reached the Supreme Court. The court said separate schools were unconstitutional. Brown's case was one of the first steps toward equal rights for African Americans.

Nine-year-old Linda Brown stands in front of her segregated elementary school in Kansas in 1954. She was refused admission to a white elementary school and her case went to the Supreme Court.

Engel v. Vitale (1962): **Prayer in Schools**

You may have heard the phrase "separation of church and state." Those words are not in the Constitution, but the idea is there. The First Amendment says that people may follow any religion they wish. The government may not prevent that. But it also says that the government cannot force people to follow a specific faith. The Supreme Court upheld that idea in 1962. The Court ruled that public schools are part of the government, so they cannot make students say prayers. That would be forcing them to follow one religion. This ruling was only for public schools. Private and church-based schools may have their students say prayers.

CHAPTER 5

★

State Governments

"So, now do you know the parts of government?" questioned Kelcey.

"I think so," Kylie replied. "But what about the government here in Kansas?"

"Well," said Kelcey, "Kansas also has executive, legislative, and judicial branches. In fact, all state governments are like that. But they're all different, too."

"Different how?"

"It's like basketball," Kelcey explained. "All teams play by the same rules. But no two teams play exactly the same way. All state governments have to follow the rules in the U.S. Constitution. But each state does it in a different way."

"Like, how?"

"Well," said Kelcey, "our team doesn't have any really tall players, but we're fast. So we pass the ball a lot and keep moving all the time. The team in Derby has one very tall player. She stays near the basket, and the other girls try to get the ball to her."

"I think I get it," said Kylie. "Our team has different kinds of players than Derby, so we play the game differently. Each team does what's best for them, but they both follow the rules of basketball."

Kelcey gave her sister a high five. "You have got it, Kylie," she said. "And that's how state governments work. They all have to follow the rules in the U.S. Constitution. But each state does it in a different way."

State Executive Branches

Each state has a chief executive. That person is called a governor. He or she is the highest official in a state. A governor's job is much like that of the president. He or she can name leaders of state agencies and helps make the state's budget. The governor can propose laws to the state **legislature** and can veto laws passed by the legislature.

In most states, the governor serves for four years. In New Hampshire and Vermont, the governor's term is just two years. Many states also have a lieutenant governor. That person takes over if the governor dies or is too sick to work.

Someone is out of uniform! Sarah Palin, the governor of Alaska, traveled to Kuwait in 2007. Soldiers from her state were stationed there. She visited them to learn about their mission and hear their concerns.

State Legislative Branches

Differences among state legislatures start with their names. They may be called the Legislature, the General Assembly, or the General Court. Like the U.S. Congress, nearly all state legislatures have two houses. One house is always called the Senate. The other house is known by different names in different states.

No matter what they are called, these legislatures make laws for their states. The process for making a state law is much like making a federal law in Congress. A bill is suggested in one house. It is studied, voted on, and sent to the other house. When both houses agree, the bill goes to the governor. If he or she signs the bill, it becomes a law.

STRANGE STATE LAWS

States have some pretty strange laws.

- In Hawaii, you can be fined for *not* owning a boat.
- Women in Vermont must get written permission from their husbands to wear false teeth.
- It is against the law to fish for whales—in Nebraska!
- In Georgia and New York, it is illegal to carry an ice cream cone in your pocket on Sunday.

States have a great deal of law-making freedom. This allows them to deal with local issues and problems. All state laws, however, must agree with the U.S. Constitution and with federal law.

State Judicial Branches

States have their own courts. The highest court in each state must decide if laws agree with the state constitution. In most states, this is the State Supreme Court. In New York, however, the highest court is called the Court of Appeals.

The California State Legislature meets in this building in Sacramento. The Capitol building is also a museum. It has displays of artwork and objects from California's history.

DON'T RUN IN THE HALL!

State courts handle all sorts of cases. This one began in New Jersey not long ago. It was the end of the school day. An eleven-year-old boy was afraid he would miss his bus. He ran down the hall as fast as he could. Near the doors, he bumped into a teacher, knocking her to the floor. He apologized and then got on the bus. The teacher, however, sued the boy's parents. His parents didn't tell the boy about it because they didn't want him to worry. Two years went by. A judge wanted the student to testify. The boy learned about the court case when a deputy sheriff came to his door to bring him to court!

States have lower-level courts, too. Some are criminal courts. In these courts, people accused of crimes are tried by a judge and jury. There are also civil courts. These courts may hear cases about traffic accidents or property ownership.

Native American Governments

Some states have large Native American populations. In these states, tribes can form their own governments. They can elect their own leaders and make their own laws. Some tribes, such as the Navajo in Arizona, even have their own police force.

Tribal laws must agree with the laws of the United States. However, tribes may be free from some state laws. In New York, for example, gambling is illegal. But Native Americans are allowed to have gambling casinos on their tribal lands.

Building and caring for parks, playgrounds, and sports fields is just one of the jobs of local governments.

Local Governments

States also have county, city, or town governments. They make laws for the people in the area. Local governments can collect taxes to help pay for schools, libraries, parks, and road repairs. Public safety is also controlled by local governments. They set up police and fire departments. Courts are part of towns and city governments, too. Local courts deal with problems such as speeding tickets and unsafe buildings.

There are executive, legislative, and judicial branches at all levels of government. When federal, state, and local governments all work together, the whole country benefits.

Glossary

appeal: a request for a legal case to be heard again by a higher court

bill: a written plan for a new law to be considered by Congress

budget: a plan for using money

cabinet: the heads of the major government departments

controversial: something that causes people to take sides or argue

counterfeit: fake

executive branch: the part of government that carries out the laws

federal: having to do with the national government of the United States

House of Representatives: one of the two houses of Congress; the number of representatives for each state is based on the state's population

impeachment: the process of formally bringing charges against a public official for doing something wrong while in office

judicial branch: the part of government that decides if laws have been followed

justice: a judge

legislative branch: the part of government that makes the laws

legislature: a group of people with the authority to make laws

oversight: watching over something with care and teaching

segregate: to keep apart from the main group

Senate: one of the two houses in Congress; each state has two senators

treaty: a formal agreement between two or more countries

U.S. Constitution: the written plan and laws of the U.S. government

veto: to reject something, such as a bill, by refusing to approve it

To Find Out More

Books

Congress. World Almanac Library of American Government (series).
Geoffrey M. Horn. (Gareth Stevens)

Don't Know Much About the Presidents. Don't Know Much About (series).
Kenneth C. Davis. (HarperCollins Children's Books)

Supreme Court. World Almanac Library of American Government (series).
Geoffrey M. Horn. (Gareth Stevens)

Web Sites

Ben Franklin's Guide to the President's Cabinet
bensguide.gpo.gov/6-8/government/national/cabinet.html

Ben Franklin's Guide to the Supreme Court
bensguide.gpo.gov/6-8/government/national/scourt.html

Congressional Quiz
www.congressforkids.net

Kids in the House: the Office of the Clerk of the House of Representatives
clerkkids.house.gov

Publisher's note to educators and parents: Our editors have carefully reviewed these web sites to ensure that they are suitable for children. Many web sites change frequently, however, and we cannot guarantee that a site's future contents will continue to meet our high standards of quality and educational value. Be advised that children should be closely supervised whenever they access the Internet.

Index

About the Author

William David Thomas lives in Rochester, New York, where he works with students who have special needs. Bill has written software documentation, training programs, books for children, speeches, advertising copy, and lots of letters. Bill claims he was once King of Fiji, but gave up the throne to pursue a career as a relief pitcher. It's not true.